I Wonder Why

The Wind Blows

and Other Questions About Our Planet

Anita Ganeri

KING*f*ISHER

NEW YORK

KINGFISHER
a Houghton Mifflin Company imprint
215 Park Avenue South
New York, New York 10003
www.houghtonmifflinbooks.com

First published in 1994
10 9 8

8TR/0602/TIM/HBM/128MA

LIBRARY OF CONGRESS CATALOGING-IN-PUBLICATION DATA
Ganeri, Anita.
    I wonder why the wind blows and other questions about
our planet/by Anita Ganeri.—1st American ed.
        p.   cm.—(I wonder why)
    Includes index.
    1. Earth—Miscellanea—Juvenile literature.
    2. Geophysics—Miscellanea—Juvenile literature.
    [1. Earth—Miscellanea. 2. Geophysics—Miscellanea]
    I. Title. II. Series: I wonder why
(New York, N. Y.)
    OB631.4.G36 1994
    550—dc20   93-48559 CIP AC

ISBN 1-85697-996-2
Printed in China

Series editor: Jackie Gaff
Series designer: David West Children's Books
Author: Anita Ganeri
Editor: Claire Llewellyn
Art editor: Christina Fraser
Illustrations (including cover): Chris Forsey;
    Tony Kenyon (B.L. Kearley) all cartoons

CONTENTS

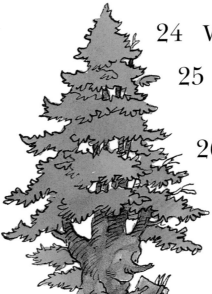

Is the Earth round?

If you were an astronaut floating around in space, the Earth would look like a gigantic ball. It isn't perfectly round, though. Like a ball that's been gently squashed, it's slightly flatter at the top and bottom, and it bulges out just a little at the middle.

● The Earth measures 24,902 miles (40,075 km) around its "waist" — the equator. If you walked night and day, it would take you more than a year to get this far!

● The Earth looks blue from space. That's because nearly three-fourths of it is covered by the sea.

Equator

The crust is the rocky layer beneath your feet.

The mantle is a thick layer of rock. It's so hot that some of the rock has melted.

The core is made of metal. The outer core is runny and liquid, but the inner core is solid.

Outer core

Inner core

● It's very hot indeed at the center of the Earth — more than 9,000°F (5000°C). That's many times hotter than a really scorching hot summer's day!

What is the Earth made of?

The Earth is made up of different layers of rock and metal. Some of the layers are hard, but others are so hot that they've melted and are runny — a bit like molasses.

● The Earth's crust doesn't stop at the seashore. It goes on under the deepest oceans.

How old is the Earth?

Scientists think the Earth formed over 4 billion years ago — although no one was there to see! They think the Moon formed then, too.

• Human beings are very new to the Earth. If you imagine our planet's 4-billion-year-long history squeezed into one year, people have only been around since late on December 31!

▽ About 200 million years ago there was just one supercontinent called Pangaea.

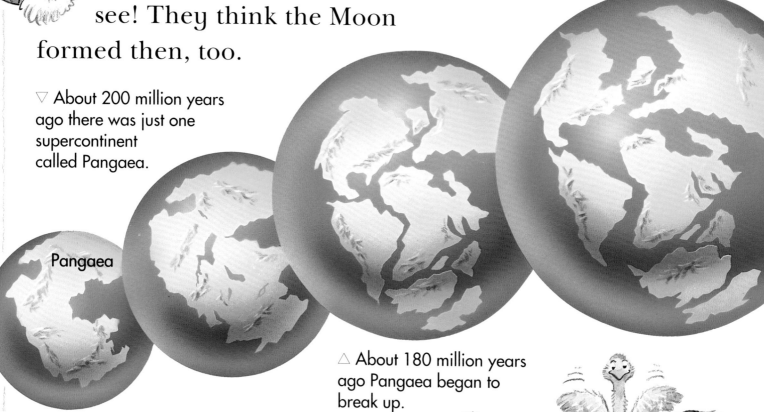

Pangaea

△ About 180 million years ago Pangaea began to break up.

• Continents are massive pieces of land. There are seven of them in all. Trace them from a map, and try to see how they once fitted together.

Asia

Europe

Africa

Australia

North America

South America

Antarctica

• Emus live in Australia, rheas in South America, and ostriches in Africa. They look similar, and none of them can fly. They may have been related to one kind of bird. It could have walked to all three continents millions of years ago, when the land was joined.

Has the Earth changed much?

Yes, it has! About 300 million years ago, most of the land was joined together in one big piece. Then it began to break up into smaller pieces called continents. These slowly drifted apart, until they reached the places they're in today.

▽ About 65 million years ago the continents drifted farther apart.

▽ Today, the continents are still drifting.

● North America and Europe are still moving apart by about 2 inches (4cm) each year. That's about the length of your thumb.

Where are the highest mountains?

● Himalaya means "home of the snows." It's a good name for these freezing peaks.

The Himalayas in Asia are the world's highest mountains. They're so high that they're known as "the roof of the world." The towering mountain peaks are bitterly cold places where the snow and ice never melt.

● These are the highest mountains on each continent:

Asia – Mt. Everest 29,028 feet

S. America – Aconcagua 22,834 feet

N. America – Mt. McKinley 20,320 feet

Africa – Mt. Kilimanjaro 19,340 feet

Europe – Mt. Elbrus 18,480 feet

Antarctica – Vinson Massif 16,860 feet

Australia – Mt. Kosciusko 7,316 feet

Can mountains shrink?

Many mountains are getting smaller all the time. Every day small chips of rock are carried away by ice, snow, and running water.

Some mountains are getting bigger though. The Himalayas are still being pushed up by movements inside the Earth.

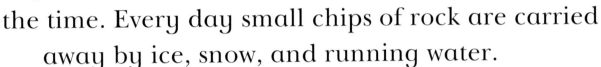

● In Hawaii there is a mountain called Mauna Kea which is more than 4,000 feet (1,300 m) higher than Mount Everest. Most of it is under the sea though.

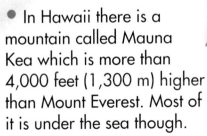

● The higher you go up a mountain, the colder it becomes. Many of the animals that live high up on mountains have thick woolly coats to keep out the cold — goats, llamas, and yaks, for example.

Which mountains breathe fire?

Volcanoes are mountains that sometimes spurt out burning ash, gas, and hot runny rock called lava. The gas and fiery lava come from deep down inside the Earth, and burst up through cracks in the crust.

● The saucerlike top of a volcano is called a crater. Sometimes a dead volcano's crater fills with rainwater and makes a beautiful lake.

● There are about 500 active volcanoes on land. There are even more under the sea.

Do people live on volcanoes?

It's a risky thing to do, but many people live on volcanoes — especially farmers. The ash from a volcano makes the soil very rich, so the farmers can grow large crops. They need to be able to run fast though!

● There are volcanoes in space, too. Olympus Mons on the planet Mars is three times higher than Earth's Mount Everest.

● Pilots beware! The ash and dust from a volcano can get inside a plane's engines and stop them dead.

What makes the Earth shake?

The Earth's surface is made up of huge pieces of hard rock which drift on the hot runny rock below. Sometimes these pieces push and shove against each other, making the Earth shake. This is what happens during an earthquake.

● In the worst earthquakes the ground cracks open, streets sink, and buildings crumble to piles of rubble.

● The greatest danger in an earthquake is a building collapsing on top of you. Taking shelter under a table or a doorway may save your life.

Can people tell if an earthquake is coming?

Scientists who study earthquakes are called seismologists. Although they know where earthquakes are likely to happen, they usually can't say exactly when.

● People have tried to design earthquake-proof buildings. Some of the latest ones are shaped like pyramids or cones.

● Animals seem to feel the land moving long before we do. Dogs howl, snakes wriggle out of their holes, and chickens run for their lives!

● The people of ancient China believed that the Earth was balanced on the shoulders of a giant ox. Earthquakes happened when the ox shifted the Earth from one shoulder to the other.

What is the Room of Candles?

Deep down below the mountain slopes of eastern Italy is a magical cave known as the Room of Candles. It gets its name from the white spikes of rock that grow up from the floor of the cave, like candles. They are really stalagmites, and they grow in small cups of rock that look like candle holders.

● Like all underground caves, the Room of Candles was made by rainwater trickling down and eating away at the rock.

● Thousands of years ago people sheltered in caves. They painted pictures of bison and woolly mammoths on the walls.

● People who like to explore the secret world of underground tunnels and caves are called spelunkers.

● Bats love the darkness of caves. They roost in them during the daytime, and they use them as nurseries for their babies.

● Don't sit and watch a stalactite grow. It can take more than 1,000 years to get half an inch (1cm) longer!

What's the difference between stalactites and stalagmites?

Stalactites and stalagmites are both long and pointed, like icicles made of rock. The only difference between them is that while stalactites grow down from the roof of a cave, stalagmites grow up from the floor.

● Who lives in dark underground caves? Lizards and worms — that's who!

Where do rivers begin?

● On some mountains, huge rivers of ice grind slowly downhill. These ice rivers are called glaciers.

Rivers start as tiny streams. Some streams begin where springs bubble out of the ground. Others form on mountains, when the tips of icy glaciers begin to melt. And some trickle out of lakes.

1 Rain falls on the hills and sinks into the ground.

2 Water trickles up out of a spring.

3 The stream joins others, and becomes a fast-flowing river.

4 The river reaches flatter land. It gets wider and flows more slowly.

Why do some rivers flow so slowly?

At the bottom of a hill, the ground becomes flatter, slowing the river down. Instead of rushing downhill in a straight line, the river flows in big bends called meanders.

Where do rivers end?

Most rivers end their journey at the sea. The mouth of the river is where fresh river water mixes with the salty water of the sea.

● Some rivers don't flow into the sea. They flow into lakes instead, or drain into the ground.

● The longest river of all is the Nile River in Egypt. It flows for 4,160 miles (6,670 km).

● The world's shortest river is the D River in Oregon. At just 120 feet (37m), it is only as long as about ten canoes.

5 A river sometimes cuts through one of its bends — leaving behind a curvy oxbow lake.

● Birds love feeding at a river mouth. They pull out the worms that live in the gooey mud!

6 At its mouth, the river joins the salty water of the sea.

How high is the sky?

The sky is part of an invisible skin of air around the Earth. This skin is called the atmosphere, and it reaches out into space for about 300 miles (500 km).

There's a very important gas called oxygen in the atmosphere — we all need to breathe oxygen to stay alive.

● The Earth is the only planet known to have enough oxygen for living things.

● If the Earth gets too hot, the ice at the Poles could melt. The seas would rise and drown many towns along the coasts.

What is the greenhouse effect?

The greenhouse effect is the name scientists have given to a hot problem. Waste gases from factories, power stations, and cars are building up in the atmosphere and trapping too much heat close to the Earth. Our planet may be getting warmer — like a greenhouse in summer.

OZONE LAYER

3 Above the planes is the ozone layer. This works a bit like a sunblock, protecting us from the Sun's burning rays.

2 Planes fly in the next layer, high above the clouds where the skies are clear. The air is thinner here, and has less oxygen in it.

1 The atmosphere is made up of different layers. In the lowest layer, the air carries clouds and weather around the Earth.

What are clouds made of?

Some clouds look like they're made of cotton balls — but they're not! Clouds are made of billions of water droplets and ice crystals. These are so tiny and light that they float in the air.

● You'd need your umbrella on Mount Waialeale in Hawaii. It rains there for 350 days each year.

● Without rain, no plants would grow. Then what would we all eat?

When does rain fall from clouds?

Rain falls when water droplets in a cloud start joining together. They get bigger and heavier until, in the end, they are too heavy to float, and fall to the ground as rain.

● Have you ever heard of showers of frogs or fish? Well, they do happen. The animals are sometimes sucked up from ponds by extra strong winds. Later on, they fall to the ground with the rain.

How cold is snow?

Snowflakes are water droplets that have frozen into crystals of ice. To stay frozen, they have to be at freezing point — that's 32°F (0°C). If they get any warmer than this, snowflakes melt and fall to the ground as rain.

● The biggest snowman ever built was more than 70 feet (22 m) high. That's about as tall as a seven-story building.

Where do thunderstorms start?

Thunderstorms start in the huge black thunderclouds that sometimes gather at the end of a hot summer's day. Inside the clouds, strong winds hurl the water droplets around, and the cloud crackles with electricity. It flashes through the sky in great dazzling sparks, which we call lightning.

● It's safest to stay inside during a thunderstorm. Never take shelter under a tree — it might get struck by lightning.

● One man was struck by lightning seven different times! Roy C. Sullivan had his hair set alight twice and his eyebrows burned off. He even lost a big toenail.

● Lightning can travel as far as 87,000 miles (140,000 km) in 1 second!

- To find out how far away a storm is, count the number of seconds between the lightning and the thunder. The storm is 1 mile (1.6 km) away for every 5 seconds you count.

- The biggest thunderclouds tower 10 miles (16 km) into the air. That's nearly twice the height of Mount Everest.

What is thunder?

Sparks of lightning are incredibly hot. As they flash through the sky, they heat the air so quickly that it makes a loud booming noise like an explosion. This is thunder.

What is a tornado?

A tornado is a spinning twist of wind that speeds across the ground, sucking up everything in its path. Tornadoes happen mainly in the United States.

Hurricanes are another kind of spinning storm, but they begin over warm tropical seas. Hurricane winds can blow at up to 150 miles (240 km) per hour.

● In 1931, a tornado lifted a train into the air and dumped it in a ditch.

• Air is invisible, so you can't see the wind. But you can feel it on your face, and see how it makes the trees sway.

Why does the wind blow?

When you feel the wind blow, it's because air is on the move. Air moves when it's warm. It gets lighter and it rises up into the sky. Cooler air then rushes in to take its place, making a breeze.

• Here's proof that warm air rises. Put a feather over a hot radiator and watch it float upward on the rising air.

How often does it rain in a rain forest?

It rains almost every day in a rain forest, but it doesn't pour all day long. The air gets hotter and hotter, and stickier and stickier, until there's a heavy thunderstorm in the afternoon. After that, it's dry again.

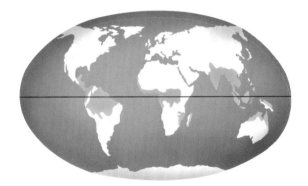

● The world's biggest rain forest is in South America. It stretches for thousands of miles along the banks of the Amazon River.

Where are rain forests?

The places where rain forests grow are shown above in green. These are the world's warmest areas, near the equator.

● Anacondas are enormous snakes. They hide in the muddy waters of the Amazon, waiting for a tasty meal to pass by.

- Rain forests are home to over half of all the animals and plants that live on Earth.

- This book started life as a tree trunk! Most paper comes from coniferous trees, such as spruce and pine.

Where is the biggest forest?

The world's biggest forest stretches right across the top of Europe and Asia. The trees in this forest are conifers — they have hard narrow leaves called needles.

- Brown bears and wolves live in the dark forests of the north. Reindeer shelter there during the long cold winters.

Where does it never rain?

Deserts are the driest places in the world. In some deserts it never rains at all. In others, there isn't any rain for months or years on end. Deserts are very windy, too. The wind blows the sand up into big piles, called dunes.

● The Atacama Desert in Chile, South America, is the world's driest desert. It had no rain for 400 years. Then, in 1971, it suddenly poured.

● Many people who live in deserts are nomads. They move from place to place with their animals, looking for food and water.

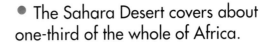

- The Sahara Desert covers about one-third of the whole of Africa.

Which is the sandiest desert?

The Sahara Desert in North Africa is the biggest desert in the world. Huge parts of it are covered with rolling hills of sand. Desert land isn't always sandy, though. A lot of it is rocky, or covered with stones and gravel.

- The highest sandcastle ever built stood as tall as three people.

- Sand blown by the wind can strip paint off a car like a giant sheet of sandpaper.

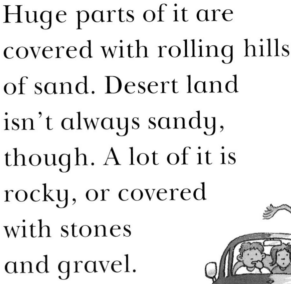

How hot are deserts?

In the hottest desert the temperature can rise to a scorching 120°F (50°C), and there's not a bit of shade. But once the sun sets, the desert cools down.

What's it like at the Poles?

The North and South Poles are at the very ends of the Earth. They are freezing cold places with biting winds. Ice and snow stretch as far as the eye can see — not the best place for a vacation!

● Polar bears live at the North Pole, and penguins live at the South Pole. They never get the chance to meet!

● Antarctica is a huge ice-covered continent around the South Pole. In places, the ice is nearly 3 miles (5 km) thick.

Which is the coldest place in the world?

Vostok Station is a really chilly spot in Antarctica. The temperature here is usually about -72°F (-58°C), but it has dropped to -128°F (-89°C) — the coldest ever known!

● Mount Erebus must be the warmest spot in Antarctica. It's an active volcano!

Where do polar bears live?

Polar bears live around the Arctic Ocean, near the North Pole. Strangely enough, they've never lived in Antarctica, though there's plenty of food and just as much snow and ice there.

● Icebergs float in the sea. They were once part of rivers of ice called glaciers.

● Polar bears never slip on the ice. The rough skin and hair on the soles of their feet give them a bit of extra grip.

Index